H is for Home Run

A Baseball Alphabet

Written by Brad Herzog and Illustrated by Melanie Rose

Sleeping Bear Press™

315 E. Eisenhower Parkway, Ste. 200
Ann Arbor, MI 48108
www.sleepingbearpress.com

Sleeping Bear Press is an imprint of Gale, a part of Cengage Learning.

Printed and bound in the United States.

10 9 8 7 6 (case)
10 9 8 7 6 5 4 (pbk)

Library of Congress Cataloging-in-Publication Data

Herzog, Brad.
H is for home run : a baseball alphabet / written by Brad Herzog;
illustrated by Melanie Rose.
p. cm.

case ISBN: 978-1-58536-219-6   **pbk** ISBN: 978-1-58536-475-6

1. Baseball—Juvenile literature. 2. Alphabet books—Juvenile literature.
[1. Baseball. 2. Alphabet.] I. Rose, Melanie, ill. II. Title.
GV867.5.H46 2004
796.357—dc22   2003025874

To Carl Berg, teacher and pitcher.

BRAD

❧

To grandparents everywhere, especially my 97-year-old grandma,
Florence Black, who loves watching all manner of sports on the telly.

MELANIE

A is for Abner Doubleday. Many people believe he invented baseball in 1839 in Cooperstown, New York. In fact, that is why the National Baseball Hall of Fame was located there a century later. But historians now believe Doubleday had nothing to do with the game's origins. Baseball actually evolved from a British game called rounders. In 1845 another **A**—Alexander Cartwright—organized the Knickerbocker Base Ball Club of New York, a team that compiled the first known set of baseball rules in America.

The All-Star Game is an exhibition contest played at midseason between the top players from major league baseball's two leagues, the American League and the National League. The first All-Star Game was played in 1933. Fans vote for the starting lineups.

Another **A** is Hank Aaron. He spent 23 seasons in the major leagues, 21 of them with the Milwaukee and Atlanta Braves. The right-handed hitting outfielder retired in 1976 with a record 755 home runs.

Aa

A

A is for the all-stars—
baseball's acrobatic aces,
who throw and catch and hit
and run around the bases.

George Herman "Babe" Ruth was known as "The Bambino" and "The Sultan of Swat." The burly outfielder slugged 714 homers in his career. His 60 home runs in 1927 were more than the total of 12 different teams!

B is also for the bat, the ball, and the bases. Some bats are aluminum, but most are made from northern white ash trees. Major leaguers generally prefer bats measuring 33 to 35 inches long. The longest bats allowed are 42 inches in the major leagues and 33 inches in Little League. The ball is made of two pieces of cowhide stitched together over tightly wound yarn. The bases are square canvas bags filled with sawdust or sand and measuring either 14 inches (in Little League) or 15 inches (in the big leagues) on each side. Of course, in a pickup baseball game between friends, anything can serve as a base—a jacket, a scrap of cardboard, even a baseball glove.

B b

B is for the best—Babe Ruth,
        the New York Yankee great
who batted balls toward bleachers
        at a then-unheard-of rate.

C c

C is for clutch cleanup hitters
who crush a curveball—CRACK!—
and tip their caps for curtain calls,
the crowd calling them back.

The cleanup hitter bats fourth in a team's lineup. If the three previous batters have reached base, the cleanup hitter can "clean up" the bases with a hit to score the runners. Often he is the team's best hitter. One of the best ever was another **C**—Ty Cobb, who compiled a record career batting average of .367. Batting average is figured by dividing a player's total hits by his total times at bat.

Unlike a fastball, which is a straight pitch thrown with great speed, a curveball curves as it reaches the plate. Other trick pitches include a slider (which looks like a fastball but curves sharply), a knuckleball (which moves unpredictably), and a changeup (a slow pitch to throw off a batter's timing).

Another **C** is the cycle, a difficult feat in which a player hits a single (one-base hit), a double (two-base hit), a triple (three-base hit), and a home run (four-base hit) in the same game.

D is for the diamond,
      a delightful design
   that gives us daring double plays
      and doubles down the line.

A baseball field is called a diamond because the infield is a square turned on its edge with a base located at each corner. **D** is also for dugouts. Generally, the home team's dugout is on the third-base side of the diamond and the visiting team's is on the first-base side.

The double play is a fielding play in which two outs are recorded. It might be an infielder "forcing out" a player at second base before throwing out the batter at first base. Or it might be an outfielder catching a fly ball and then throwing out a runner trying to advance to the next base. It might even happen when a batter strikes out while a runner is caught stealing.

D is also for designated hitter (DH). Since 1973 the American League has used a DH in the lineup to bat in place of the pitcher. In the National League and Little League the pitcher bats for himself.

E e

E is for an error,
a fielder's—oops!—mistake,
and games in extra innings
that keep us wide-awake.

Baseball games have no time clock. Games end after nine innings (six innings in Little League), but if the score is tied the teams keep playing extra innings until one team outscores the other. So it is possible for a game to go on...and on...and on. The longest major league game that didn't end in a tie took place in 1984. It began on May 8 and was completed on May 9. The Chicago White Sox finally beat the Milwaukee Brewers on a home run by Harold Baines in the 25th inning!

An error is a misplay by a fielder, such as a dropped fly ball or an inaccurate throw, that allows a runner to reach base, advance an extra base, or score.

E is also for ERA, which stands for earned run average. It measures the average number of earned runs (runs scored without the benefit of an error) that a pitcher allows per nine innings.

F is for a fly ball
    floating freely in the air.
Who can figure where it falls?
    It might be foul or fair.

A fly ball can be caught in fair or foul territory. Either way, the batter is out. To prevent a collision, the proper fielder often shouts, "I got it!" If there is a runner on base, the fielder who catches the ball must make a decision. He can throw the ball to the next base, trying to prevent the runner from advancing. Or he can fire it to a "cut-off man," an infielder who then throws it to the proper base.

F is also a full count. The count is the number of balls and strikes a batter has against him. A full count means three balls (pitches out of the strike zone) and two strikes (foul balls or pitches in the strike zone). If the next pitch is ball four, the batter is awarded a base on balls (also called a "walk") and trots to first base. If the next pitch is a strike, the batter is out.

Ff

G is for a grand slam,
   a bases-loaded clout
that clears the big Green Monster—
   over, up, and out.

The grand slam is one of the most dramatic feats in sports. A home run with the bases loaded (runners on first base, second base, and third base) scores four runs. The Green Monster is the famous left field wall in Boston's Fenway Park. It is 37 feet high, 240 feet long, 310 feet from home plate, and painted a special color called Fence Green.

G is also for gloves. The earliest baseball gloves covered only the palm of the hand. In fact, some fielders didn't wear a glove at all. In modern baseball a player's fielding position determines his glove size. Outfielders' gloves tend to be larger so they can reach farther. A first baseman's glove is long and wide to help him scoop up wild throws. The catcher wears a round, padded glove to protect his hand from fast pitches. The last major leaguer to field without a glove was third baseman Jerry Denny, who retired in 1894.

Gg

H is for home plate
and hitting homers. Wow!
Then happy home announcers
shout, "A home run! Holy Cow!"

In the early days of baseball, home plate was actually a circular iron plate painted white. Then it became a square. In 1900 the modern shape was introduced—a five-sided rubber slab 17 inches wide and 17 inches deep. On each side of home plate is a rectangular batter's box measuring four feet by six feet. The batter must stand inside it while hitting.

There are two kinds of home runs in baseball. Most common is when a ball is hit over the outfield fence. The batter is awarded a four-base hit and can jog around the bases. But an inside-the-park home run is when the batter speeds all the way around the bases before the fielders can tag him out.

H is also for helmets. Players wear baseball caps when they are fielding, but hitters wear batting helmets for safety. Often, when there is a wild pitch, the helmet prevents serious head injury.

Although he was often overshadowed by his teammate Babe Ruth, Lou Gehrig was a Hall of Fame first baseman with the New York Yankees. The "Iron Horse" is best remembered for his amazing endurance streak. From June 2, 1925 through May 2, 1939, he appeared in 2,130 straight major league games. Most people thought it was an unbreakable record until Baltimore Orioles shortstop Cal Ripken Jr. played in 2,632 games in a row from 1982 to 1998. Ripken's streak included an even more incredible run of 8,243 consecutive innings!

Sadly, soon after Gehrig's streak ended he discovered that he had an incurable illness called amyotrophic lateral sclerosis. It is now known as "Lou Gehrig's Disease." He retired in a special ceremony in Yankee Stadium. Looking back on his life and career, he told the packed stadium, "Today, I consider myself the luckiest man on the face of the Earth."

I i

I is for the Iron Horse—
Lou Gehrig was his name,
the youngest man ever
elected to the Hall of Fame.

J j

J is for Jackie Robinson,
    who stood for what was right—
to judge on someone's talent,
    not if they're black or white.

For many decades major league baseball didn't allow African-Americans to compete. But in 1945, Brooklyn Dodgers president Branch Rickey signed Jackie Robinson to a contract. In his first game with the minor league Montreal Royals in 1946, Robinson stole two bases, collected three runs batted in and had four hits, including a home run. By the end of the season he led the league in batting average (.349) and runs scored (113).

In April 1947, Robinson began playing for the Dodgers. This made him the first African-American major leaguer in the twentieth century. He won the Rookie of the Year award that season. Fifteen years later, after showing tremendous courage and changing sports forever, he was elected to the National Baseball Hall of Fame.

Another Hall of Fame ballplayer named Robinson—Frank Robinson—broke barriers, too. When he was named the player-manager of the Cleveland Indians in 1975, he became the first African-American to manage a major league team.

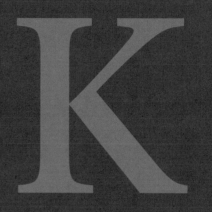

K is for kids everywhere
who keep their baseball cards
and kiss the ball goodbye
over the fence in their backyards.

Baseball cards were first produced nationally in the 1880s, when they were printed by tobacco companies. Many people simply like to trade baseball cards with their friends, but others collect them for their value. The most valuable card of all is a 1909 card of Hall of Fame shortstop Honus Wagner. It sold for more than $1 million in 2000!

K is also a symbol for a strikeout when a fan is keeping score of a baseball game. Using a scorecard, a person can keep track of every play. When scoring a game, a numbering system is used to describe playing positions—pitcher (1), catcher (2), first baseman (3), second baseman (4), third baseman (5), shortstop (6), leftfielder (7), centerfielder (8) and rightfielder (9). So an error by the leftfielder might be recorded as E7. A double play that goes from the shortstop to the second baseman to the first baseman is a 6-4-3 DP.

In 1939 Carl Stotz organized a baseball program for boys in Williamsport, Pennsylvania. There were 41 kids on three teams. There are now more than 7,400 Little League programs in more than 100 countries around the world. It is the world's largest organized youth sports program. Each summer teams from all over the globe travel to Williamsport to compete in the Little League World Series.

Little League baseball is played mostly by boys between the ages of 9 and 12, although there have been hundreds of girls who have competed over the years. Many major league players started their baseball careers in Little League. In fact, in 2003 catcher Gary Carter became the 12th former Little League player to be elected to the National Baseball Hall of Fame. Little League is about having fun, not winning and losing. Rules require that every child must play in every game.

L is local Little Leaguers
lacing up their shoes.
It's letting yourself love the game
whether you win or lose.

L l

M m

It is the manager's responsibility to develop the skills of his players, motivate them, select a batting order and call certain plays in certain situations. In most forms of organized baseball the manager is called a coach. But major league teams have several coaches who assist the manager. These include a pitching coach, hitting coach, and coaches who stand near first base and third base to advise the players when to run.

M is also for muscular home run hitters Mark McGwire, Mickey Mantle, and Willie Mays. In 1998 McGwire set a single-season record by hitting 70 homers. Mantle and Mays were both centerfielders in New York in the 1950s. They combined to hit 1,196 career home runs.

Another **M** is the minor leagues, where professional baseball players develop their skills and attempt to make it to the major leagues. There are nearly 200 minor league teams in North America.

N is the national pastime,
played in the summer heat.
It's a thrilling no-hitter, too,
quite a nifty feat.

N
n

A no-hitter is when a pitcher or a series of pitchers completes nine innings without allowing a hit. There have been more than 225 no-hitters in the major leagues since 1893, the year the pitcher's mound was finally moved to its present position 60 feet and six inches from home plate. Another **N**, Nolan Ryan, holds the record with an amazing seven no-hitters in his career.

N is also names and numbers. Numbers on the backs of uniforms didn't become popular until the New York Yankees started using them in 1929. The 1960 Chicago White Sox were the first team to display players' last names on uniforms.

Another **N** is the Negro leagues. From 1920 to 1960, African-American baseball players competed in their own professional leagues, which featured some of the most talented players in the game. Two of the Negro leagues' greatest stars were home-run-hitting catcher Josh Gibson and pitcher Leroy "Satchel" Paige.

There is always something special about Opening Day, which usually comes at the beginning of April. It could be the excitement of joining tens of thousands of people to welcome the arrival of spring. The outfield grass seems the greenest of greens, the smell of hot dogs and peanuts wafts through the stadium, and sometimes even the president of the United States is on hand to throw out the ceremonial first pitch. Best of all, everyone believes this is finally the year their favorite team will win it all!

Outs are most often made by getting three strikes, hitting a ball that is caught in the air, being forced to run to a base that has been touched by a player holding the ball, or being tagged with the ball while off base.

Another **O** is Sadaharu Oh, who has been called the "Japanese Babe Ruth." Playing in the Japan League, Oh hit 868 home runs in his career.

O is for Opening Day
when the season starts anew.
Three strikes you're out, three outs per inning
and three outfielders, too.

P is a play at the plate.
Is he safe or out?
And it's for the words "Play ball!"
That's what it's all about.

Pp

When the fielding team is in place, and the first batter of the game is ready to take his turn at bat, the home plate umpire will often shout, "Play ball!" They are two of the happiest words in sports.

A play at the plate can be one of the more exciting situations in baseball. An outfielder or cutoff man throws the ball toward the catcher, who must do several things. He must catch the ball, block home plate, and tag out the base runner, who is trying to score. Perhaps the runner and catcher collide. Does the catcher hang on to the ball? "Out!" shouts the umpire. Or maybe the runner beats the throw with a sensational slide. "Safe!" declares the ump, spreading his arms wide.

P is also for pinch hitter, when one batter substitutes for another batter in the lineup. Often this happens late in a game, when the team needs an important hit.

The stolen base is an important part of baseball. Any player on base may take off running toward the next base while a pitcher is throwing the ball toward home plate. The catcher must catch the ball and throw it to a waiting fielder, who tries to tag the player out. Stealing second base (from first base) is common. Stealing third base is less common. A steal of home happens only rarely. Rickey Henderson holds major league records for most stolen bases in a season (130) and career (more than 1,400).

Two important ways that pitchers try to prevent runners from stealing bases are pickoffs and pitchouts. A pickoff move is when the pitcher tries to surprise the runner by throwing to the base instead of toward home plate. A pitchout is when the pitcher purposely throws a ball out of the strike zone, so the catcher can more easily throw out a runner attempting to steal.

Q is when a base runner
moves at a quick pace.
Quietly, he has a quest—
stealing second base.

R is for runs, of course.
Scoring is the aim.
And it's a relief pitcher
trying to save the game.

Scoring runs, by advancing around the four bases, is the object of baseball. Babe Ruth holds the record for most runs scored in a major league season (177 in 1921). A batter is credited with a run batted in (RBI) if he makes a hit, out, or base on balls that allows a runner to score. Hack Wilson of the Chicago Cubs collected a record 191 RBIs in 1930.

The relief pitcher, or reliever, replaces a starting pitcher on the mound. Usually it is because the manager thinks a fresh arm will benefit the team. In modern major league baseball, certain pitchers are substituted only in late-game situations. These pitchers are often called stoppers. Their goal is to maintain a lead in a close game. If they do it, they are awarded a save. Lee Smith holds the major league record with 478 saves.

Rr

Stickball is a popular form of baseball played on city streets or empty paved schoolyards. The bat is a stick or broom handle, and the ball is a small rubber ball. Manhole covers may serve as bases, and cars and walls are foul lines.

Softball, invented in 1887, is related to baseball. Softball uses most of the rules of baseball, except the balls are larger, the bases are closer together, the games are seven innings long, and the pitchers throw underhand.

A bunt in baseball is a soft hit resulting from the batter holding the bat out and letting the ball hit it. A sacrifice bunt is intended to advance runners to another base at the expense of the batter, who expects to be thrown out. A squeeze play, a bunt with a runner on third base, is designed to advance the runner home.

S can be for stickball,
played on city streets,
a sacrifice, a squeeze play,
and summer bleacher seats.

T-ball, or tee ball, teaches young players (ages 4 to 8) the fundamentals of baseball. More than two million kids play the game, and nearly one-third of them are girls. Members of two teams take turns hitting a ball off a batting tee set on home plate. The ball is softer than a normal baseball, and unless it travels more than 10 feet it is a foul ball. Bases are only 50 feet apart, and there are no walks or strikeouts. A standard game lasts four innings, and an inning is over when all the players have batted once.

It has become a tradition in recent decades for the crowd to sing "Take Me Out to the Ballgame" during the seventh inning stretch (the middle of the seventh inning). The words to the song were written in 1908 by Jack Norworth, and the music was composed by Harry von Tilzer. Neither man had ever attended a baseball game!

T t

T-ball is where many kids
learn to field and swing.
And T is "Take Me Out to the Ballgame,"
which all fans love to sing.

U is for the umpire,
whose uniform is blue.
　　Right or wrong, he makes the calls
and misses but a few.

Umpires are often called the "men in blue," even though women have also been umpires. Umps control the game by making judgments such as whether a pitch is a strike or a ball, whether a batted ball is fair or foul, and whether a runner is safe or out. Umpires use hand signals when they make their calls. These signals were first used in the 1890s for the benefit of a hearing impaired player named William Hoy.

There are usually two umpires in Little League baseball games—one observing plays in the infield and one calling balls and strikes at home plate. The major leagues use four umpires for regular season games—a home plate umpire and umpires at first base, second base, and third base. Umpires in left field and right field are added during the playoffs. Professional umpires first must attend an umpire school, which usually lasts about five weeks.

U u

V is for the visiting team,
        whose uniforms are grayer,
and for a fellow voted the
        Most Valuable Player.

V

For more than a century, the home major
league baseball team has worn a mostly
white uniform, while the visiting team's
uniform is either gray or a darker color.
The visiting team always bats first—in the
top of the inning. The home team bats in
the bottom of the inning. Every big-league
team plays 81 home games and 81 road
games each season.

Since 1931 the major league baseball writ-
ers have voted to select the Most Valuable
Player (MVP) in each league. Seven men
have won the award three times. One man
has won the National League Most Valuable
Player award six times. He is Barry Bonds,
who slugged a record 73 home runs during the 2001 season.

Wrigley Field, home of the Chicago Cubs, is the oldest ballpark in the National League, dating back to 1914. Its scoreboard is still operated by hand, and it didn't even have permanent lights for night games until 1988. The famous ivy growing on Wrigley Field's outfield wall was planted in 1937.

The World Series is the championship series matching the winners of the National League and the American League. The first team to win four out of a maximum seven games is crowned the world champion. The Boston Pilgrims beat the Pittsburgh Pirates in the first World Series in 1903.

W is also for women. The All-American Girls Professional Baseball League existed from 1943 to 1954. More than 600 women competed in the league, which started with four teams but eventually had as many as ten. The rules were slightly different from those of major league baseball, including a larger ball and a shorter distance between the bases.

W is Wrigley Field
with ivy on the wall
and the wondrous World Series,
the classic every fall.

X is for the Expos,
the team from Montreal.
And the first Canadian club
to play major league ball.

In 1969 the Montreal Expos became the first major league team to play its home games outside of the United States. Thirty-four years later the Expos achieved another first—playing 22 games on the island of Puerto Rico. The Expos were considered the home team, even though Puerto Rico is more than 2,000 miles from Montreal. The Toronto Blue Jays were the second Canadian team to join the major leagues (in 1977). In 1992 Toronto became the first club from Canada to win the World Series.

X also marked the spot where Ferguson Jenkins placed his pitches. Jenkins is the only pitcher in major league history to strike out more than 3,000 batters and walk fewer than 1,000. Although more than 200 Canadian-born players have made it to the major leagues, he is the only Canadian in the National Baseball Hall of Fame. In 2001 Jenkins was named the first commissioner of the Canadian Baseball League, an independent minor league.

Y is for pitcher Cy Young,
who won and won and won—
511 victories
by the time he was done.

After every season, the Cy Young Award
is given to the best pitcher in each league.
In 22 major league seasons from 1890 to
1911, Denton True "Cy" Young pitched an
incredible 7,356 innings and won 511 games.
It is likely neither record will ever be broken.
Today, pitchers may win the Cy Young Award
with 20 wins in a season. But Cy Young did
that 15 times during his long career.

Y is also for the New York Yankees, the
most successful team in major league
history. Babe Ruth led the Yankees to their
first championship in 1923. Since then, the
team has won nearly one-third of all World
Series played—26 championships over 80
years. In 1998 the Yankees won 125
games (including the playoffs), a single-
season record.

Z is for all zeroes—
　　　　a rare feat with a name.
No hits, no runs, no errors.
　　　　　It is a perfect game.

130
000

The perfect game—pitching a complete game while your team allows no hits, no runs, and no errors—is one of baseball's rarest accomplishments. The first perfect game was pitched by a man named Lee Richmond on June 12, 1880. The second occurred just five days later. But over the next 122 years, it officially happened only 13 more times during the regular season. The most famous perfect game ever was the only one pitched during the postseason. Don Larsen of the New York Yankees pitched the only perfect game of post-season play. He achieved this feat against the Brooklyn Dodgers in Game 5 of the 1956 World Series.

Z
z
z

Brad Herzog

Brad Herzog's first published story was an article for his high school newspaper about his evening as an honorary batboy for the Chicago White Sox. He has been writing about baseball ever since. The 35-year-old freelance writer's hundreds of magazine articles have included stories examining everything from foul balls to free stadium views. A past Grand Gold Medal Award winner from the Council for Advancement and Support of Education, Brad has written more than a dozen fiction and nonfiction children's books, including *K is for Kick: A Soccer Alphabet*, also published by Sleeping Bear Press.

Melanie Rose

Melanie lives in Mississauga, Canada, with her son Liam and their two cats, Mickey and Meesha. Melanie also illustrated *M is for Maple: A Canadian Alphabet*, *Z is for Zamboni: A Hockey Alphabet*, and *K is for Kick: A Soccer Alphabet*. She is a graduate of the Ontario College of Art.